WHY SHOULD I SAVE ENERGY?

an imprint of Hodder Children's Books

WHY SHOULD I?

WHY SHOULD I Save Water?
WHY SHOULD I Save Energy?
WHY SHOULD I Protect Nature?
WHY SHOULD I Recycle?

Published in Great Britain in 2001 by Hodder Wayland,
an imprint of Hodder Children's Books
© Copyright 2001 Hodder Wayland

Commissioning editor: Vicky Brooker
Editor: Liz Gogerly
Designer: Jean Wheeler
Digital Colour: Carl Gordon

Produced in association with WWF-UK.
WWF-UK registered charity number 1081247.
A company limited by guarantee number
4016725. Panda device © 1986 WWF ®
WWF registered trademark owner.

**British Library Cataloguing in
Publication Data**
Green, Jen, 1955–
Why should I save energy?
1.Energy conservation
I.Title II.Gordon, Mike, 1948– III.Save energy?
333.7'916

ISBN 0 7502 3688 4

Printed and bound in Italy by G. Canale &
C.Sp.A., Turin

Hodder Children's Books
A division of Hodder Headline Limited
338 Euston Road, London NW1 3BH

WHY SHOULD I SAVE ENERGY?

Written by Jen Green

Illustrated by Mike Gordon

an imprint of Hodder Children's Books

In my family, we're careful how we use energy.

We never used to be careful – we wasted lots of energy. We used the car all the time.

5

We always left the lights on,

we turned the
heating on full blast,

and we all had lovely
hot baths with the
water nearly up
to the top.

Mmmmmm!

One evening my friend, Robert, was playing round at our house.

I thought electricity was always right there whenever we needed it.

Robert said that we must save energy.

Why should I save energy?

Robert knew about energy because
he had learned about it at school.

STEAM

BURNING FUEL

'Electricity is energy made by burning fuel – that's coal, oil and gas,' said Robert.

14

'Cars, trains and buses
also run on fuel.'

15

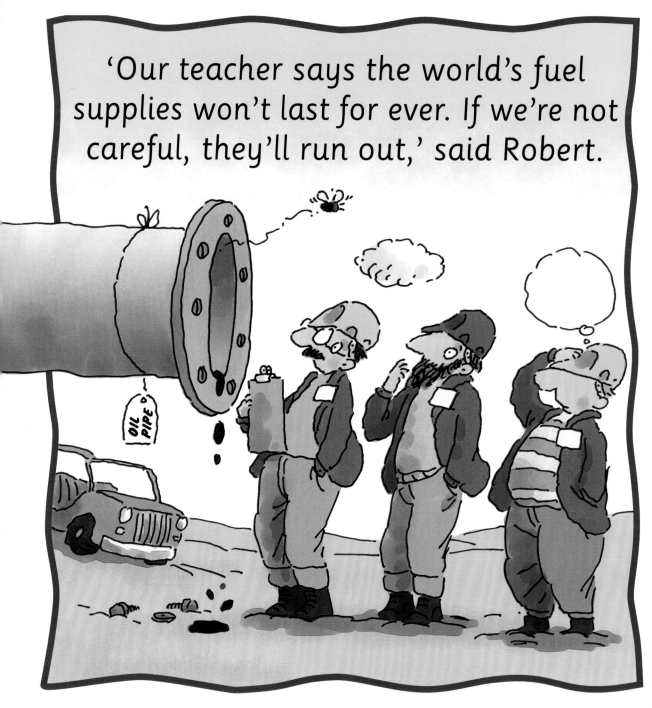

Then he said, 'What do you think would happen if our homes ran out of energy?'

'There would be no power for cooking or heating. We'd get cold – and all our food would be cold, too!'

'Buses and trains wouldn't run,
so people couldn't
get around,

and nothing would reach the shops.'

22

23

'There are loads of ways to save energy!' said Robert.
'Turn off lights when you don't need them,

close windows and
doors when the
heating is on,

and try putting a jumper
on if you feel cold rather
than the heating.'

25

'Going to school by bus or train
uses less fuel than going by car.

You could go by bike or walk,' said Robert.

Robert was right!
Saving energy is easy.
And you might find yourself
doing new
things.

Saving energy saves money too ... so you can have extra treats now and then!

Notes for parents and teachers

Why Should I? and the National Curriculum

The *Why Should I?* series satisfies a number of requirements for the *Personal, Social and Health Education* framework at Key Stage 1. There are four titles about the environment in the series: *Why Should I: Save Water? Save Energy? Protect Nature?* and *Recycle?* Within the category of *Citizenship*, these books will help young readers to think about simple environmental issues, and other social and moral dilemmas they may come across in everyday life. Within the category of *Geography*, the books will help children to understand environmental change and how to recognize it in their own surroundings, and also help them to discover how their environment may be improved and sustained. Within the category *Developing confidence and responsibility*, thinking about saving energy will also teach children to consider others, to act unselfishly and share.

Why Should I Save Energy? introduces the subject of energy as a resource, and how it can be used either wastefully or wisely. The book introduces a number of simple tasks that children can carry out to help save energy.

Suggestions for reading the book with children

As you read the book with children, you may find it helpful to stop and discuss issues as they come up in the text. Children might like to reread the story, taking on the role of different characters. Which character in the book mirrors their own attitude to energy most closely? How do their own ideas differ from those expressed in the book?

Discussing the subject of energy may introduce children to a number of unfamiliar words, including draughty, energy, environment, fuel, fossil fuels, meter, mining, petrol, pollution, power station, precious. Make a list of all the new words and discuss what they mean.

Suggestions for follow-up activities

Discuss the various forms of energy we come across in everyday life. Coal, oil and natural gas are fossil fuels (so-called because they are derived from the fossilized remains of prehistoric plants) that are burned to generate electricity. Most cars and other vehicles run on fuels (petrol, diesel) made from oil. Batteries store energy. Electricity can also be generated using nuclear power, or by harnessing the energy of sunlight, winds, waves or running water. These last resources are called renewable resources because, unlike fossil fuels, they will not run out.

Encourage children to make a list of all the things we use energy for, at home, at school and also in the wider world. Children could inspect electricity or gas meters at home or at school; most meters provide a graphic illustration of how fast energy is being used!

The book suggests a number of things that might happen if local energy supplies ran out. Children might have their own ideas about what could happen and how an energy shortage would affect them. In the wider world, energy is also vital in farming and industry. The book makes a number of suggestions about how energy can be saved. What other ideas can children come up with for saving energy?

Books to read

Spaceship Earth: Get Switched On! by Thompson Yardley (Cassell, 1992) A cartoon book that explains all about energy and how it is wasted, and includes practical ideas for saving energy.

First Starts: Saving Energy by Jacqueline Dineen (Watts Books, 1994) This information book for young readers introduces energy and its uses, and also includes energy-saving ideas.

Science All Around Me: Electricity by Karen Bryant-Mole
(Heinemann, 1988) A simple information book for younger children which explains what electricity is and how it is produced.

How Green Are You? by David Bellamy (Frances Lincoln) A cartoon book by a well-known nature expert, which explains all about the natural world and how we can help to preserve it.

You'd Never Believe It But ... a lightning bolt is hotter than the Sun and other facts about electricity (Aladdin, 2001) A science series with simple text, colour illustrations and fun projects for children.

What do we think about Our Environment? by Malcolm Penny
(Hodder Wayland, 1999) This information book introduces the environmental problems facing the world and the simple steps young readers can take to help to protect the environment.